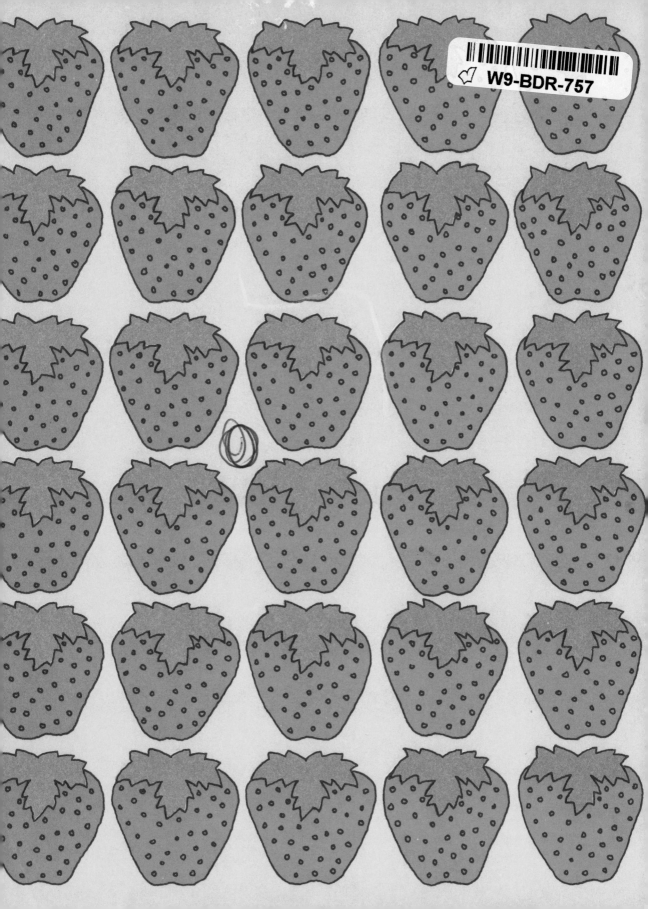

this
strawberry book
belongs to

Tim
Hoover

SOME, MORE, MOST
Copyright © 1976 by One Strawberry Inc.
All rights reserved
Printed in the United States of America
Library of Congress Catalog Card Number: 76-5776
ISBN: Trade 0-88470-022-4, Library 0-88470-023-2

Weekly Reader Books Edition

some
more
most

written by
Judy Freudberg
illustrated by
Richard Hefter

a strawberry book®

The bear is wearing some clothes.

The bear is wearing more clothes.

The bear is wearing the most clothes.

The bear is taking off most of his clothes...Whew!

Georgette Hippo is close to you.

Now Georgette is closer to you.

Georgette is now closest to you.

Some hair.

More hair.

Most hair.

Tall birds like to take baths.

Taller birds like to take baths too.

Tallest birds don't like to take baths.

Tallest birds
like showers.

Some balloons.

More balloons.

Most balloons...Bye, bye.

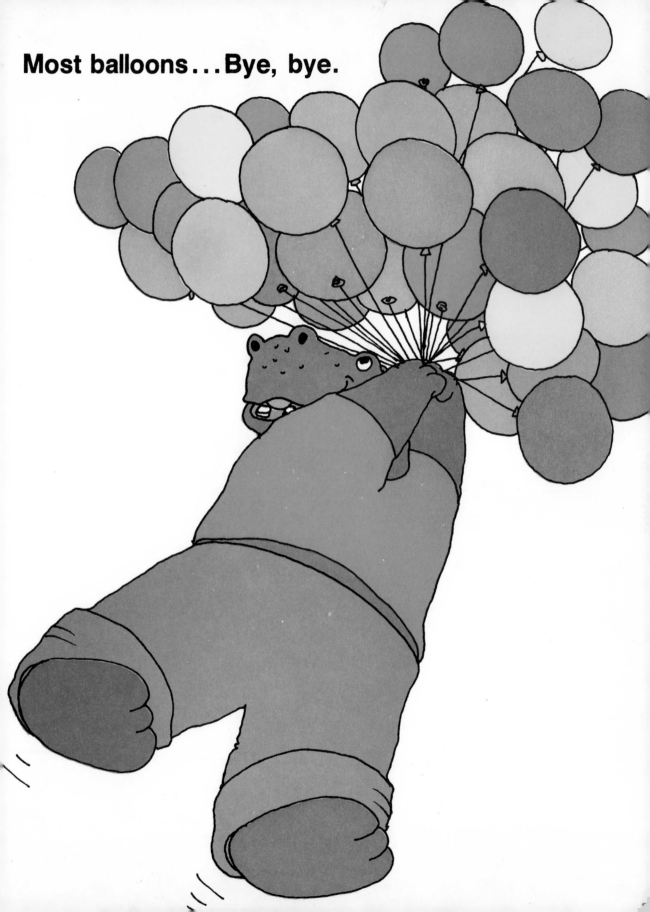

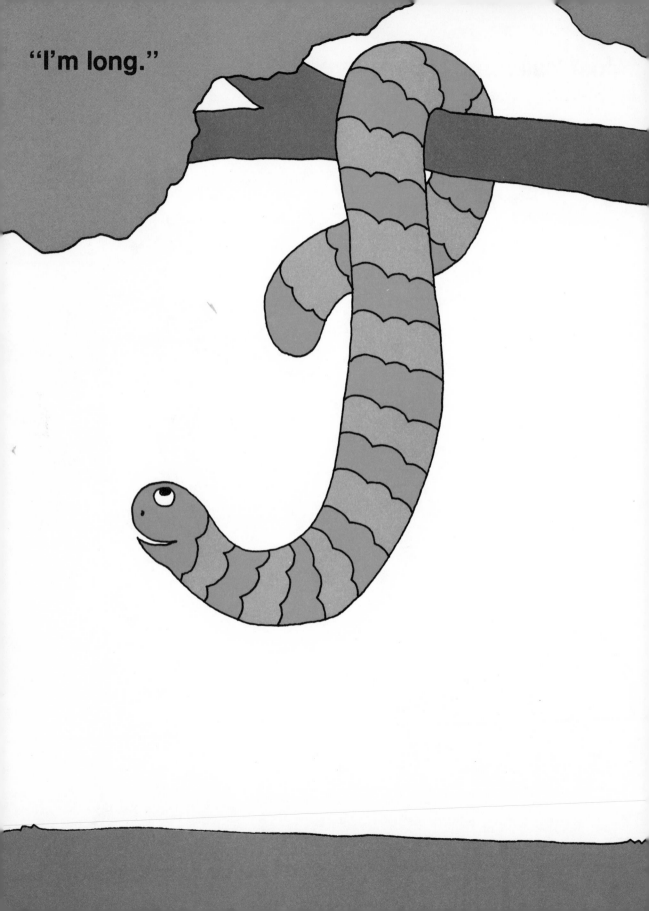

"I'm long."

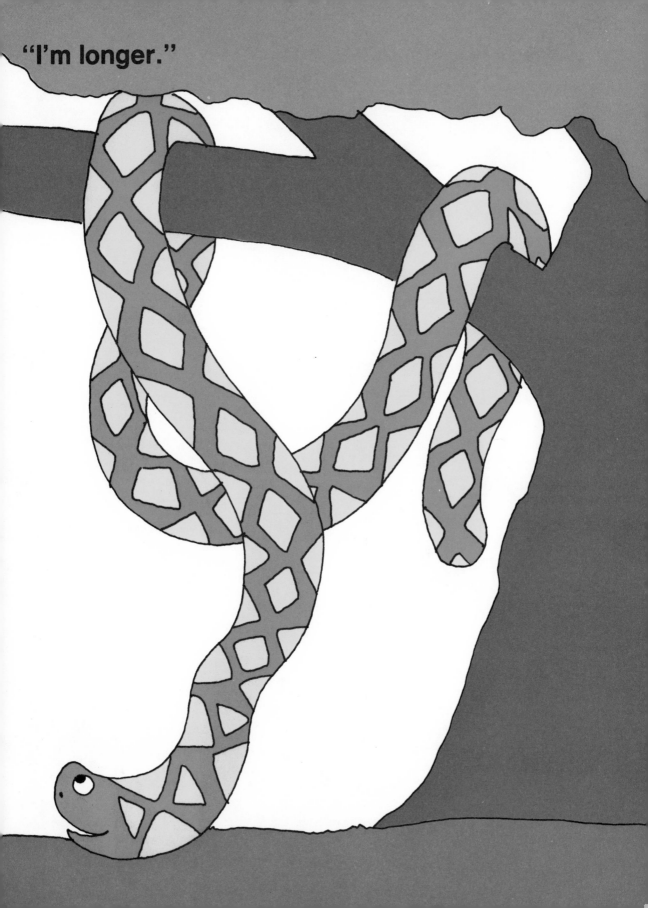

"I'm longest"..."But I don't know which end goes first."

The rabbit is eating a big cabbage.

The rabbit is eating a bigger cabbage.

The rabbit is eating the biggest cabbage.

The rabbit ate the biggest cabbage, and boy, is he full.

Some rabbits trying to see over a high fence.

More rabbits trying to see over a high fence.

The most rabbits trying to see over a high fence...
Now they are higher
than the fence.

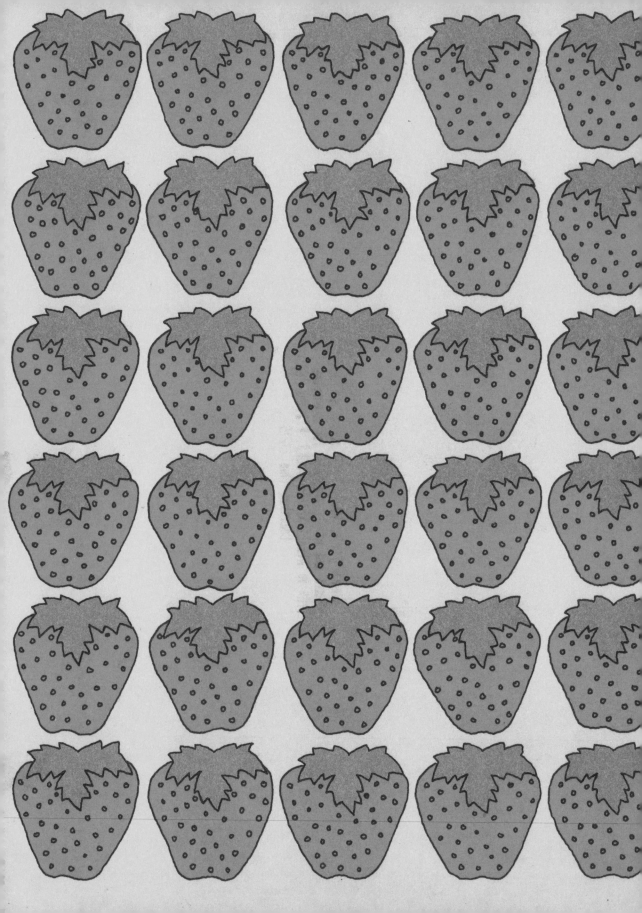